atrophy

atrophy

shilo niziolek

QUERENCIA

Querencia Press – Chicago IL

QUERENCIA PRESS

© Copyright 2023
Shilo Niziolek

ISBN 978 1 959118 67 1

www.querenciapress.com

First Published in 2023

Querencia Press, LLC
Chicago IL

Printed & Bound in the United States of America

"And in the throat a forest."
—Allison Titus, *sum of every lost ship*

Dedicated to the spoonies, the autoimmune warriors, my disability sisters and brothers. Your body, your heart, all of you is an exquisite wonder.

contents

Before

—After Emily Kendal Frey

Watched a blue heron fly underneath my body and the bridge.

Said, "No, you don't want to be inside my mind."

Met a magical old man who may or may not have turned into a bird.

Laid out on cement looking up at the giant moon and New Hampshire stars.

Heard whispers.

Spoke whispers of my own.

Hunted for turtles.

Heard an invisible girl under the bridge sing sweetly.

Wrote, My legs feel like broken matches.

Ugly cried into someone's sleeve.

Thought about the horse I used to pretend was mine.

Said, "I want to play in the god damned mud."

Wrote about things I'm tired of writing about.

Felt the sticky heat of summer press into my thighs.

Saw a skunk go running by in the darkness, its fluffy bouncing tail.

Walked barefoot through puddles and shouted, "I'm sick and tired of wearing fucking shoes."

Dreamt of the ocean.

Dreamt of sex with an older man.

Said, "I always howl at the full moon."

ROOT

The First Thirty Days

Cried while pulling the freshly washed sheets tight over the mattress.

Didn't read books.

Then, only read books.

Watched the cherry blossom turn from delicate pink buds to bursting pastel petals.

Imagined those same petals covering the ground.

Didn't write.

Didn't howl at the full pink moon.

Cried so hard in the shower that my temple throbbed the rest of the day.

Took a panic attack pill.

Watched a downy woodpecker tap on the maple in my yard.

Yelled at my partner about the possibility of dying.

Pieced together eight puzzles so that when I closed my eyes at night, my brain continued to connect puzzle pieces on the backs of my eyelids.

Smoked weed with friends on a video chat.

Talked to my therapist once a week.

Heard her say, "Living with your illness has put you in a better place than most people. You already have the processing and coping mechanisms to deal with this fear and grief."

Weeded the garden.

Thought about deep cleaning. Didn't.

Avoided the news.

Inevitably read the news and wished I hadn't.

Ordered more books, more puzzles.

Kissed my dogs. Watched my dogs play. Watched my dogs sunbathe. Listened to my dogs bark. Took photos of my dogs. Took videos of my dogs. Spooned my dogs.

Judged the people's laughter I could hear a street over at the park.

Judged the old woman munching on snacks as she walked through the grocery store while half the people around her wore gloves and masks.

Wore a mask with bunnies printed on it.

Meditated. Stopped meditating. Thought about meditating.

Built fires in the backyard, smelled the scent of smoke in my hair and on the pillows.

Nightly dreamt of scarcity.

Breathed deeply to make sure I still could.

Cleaned my whiteboard calendar off and wrote on it "the world is cancelled" instead.

Saw the largest jumping spider, asked it politely to go away.

Washed dishes. Washed more dishes. Wondered why the fuck we own so many cups and plates.

Didn't kiss my partner.

Continued to not kiss my partner.

Wished my partner would get laid off.

Memorized my credit card number, expiration date, and security code.

Almost burnt down the house by turning on the wrong burner and blackening the sky-blue pan that was sitting on it.

Stopped dreaming about sex.

Chatted on the phone with strangers for long periods of time whenever I ordered books or food from small businesses.

Drank tea.

Watched the lilacs grow, nearing bloom.

Watched multiple shows and movies that I've already seen.

Stopped crying.

Made a playlist filled with moon songs. Titled it Moon Tunes.

Bled for a week.

Climbed the walls.

Watched the grass grow.

Placed my toes in the grass.

Felt sorry for the people with kids during the pandemic.

Wished I had kids.

Realized I hate the fucking city.

Remembered that I already knew that.

Argued with my partner about selling the house when this is over and moving to the woods.

Stayed in bed a little longer, cocooned between dogs.

Listened to the cheer of the birds.

Didn't make art.

Imagined a quieter world.

A Wolf at the Door

"In me a pack of wolves appeared and disappeared / over the hills of my heart."

—Natalie Diaz, *Wolf OR-7*

Maybe it's the wolf in me, but each night as the atmosphere gets colder and my breath shoots little cloud-funnels into the threadbare thin atmosphere, I want to step out in the frigid air and howl. Last night, I sat in my living room as my dog barked at me because he wanted to play, and I howled and howled until the vibrations caused my throat to feel raw from misuse. Then my dog and I curled around each other in a pool of blankets on the couch. It's like this every winter, even when it's not yet winter.

In a few weeks, in another December, a doctor will take a metal wire and scrape cells from my cervix that have made a den, a hovel, a home, found a place where they think they belong.

And I haven't yet heard the coyotes' howl. It's the end of October, but soon. Soon. And each year at this time, I feel compelled to reach toward something. Maybe it's snow. Maybe I'll never recover myself from those diamond Wyoming landscapes reflecting the blinding blue sky for endless miles.

I wrote an entire book about desire, yet still, I am no closer to my own flesh. I strip my skin a thousand times, string it up like a canvas and place it in the museum for greedy fingers to touch.

I could run thousands of miles, over desert plains, through rivers and streams and douglas fir and snow-covered mountains.

I'm racing around the ends of Heart Mountain through the cactus and the tumbleweeds of the Wyoming plains. In me, a pack of wolves takes down the lone wandering buffalo, rose-red spray.

In me, the tainted winter snow, silent on the ground.

What I really mean when I say I hate winter is: it's cold and the remembrance of my nostril's freezing together is something I can't forget. Nor will I ever forget what it's like to fall in love under a December sky and the hollow months of January and February that fall like gray sheets of lint. There's lint in my heart and my heart stopped in a December of a different year and it's creeping ever nearer. There's something pacing around, under the sheets, outside the door, in between the linen and the lint and the thread.

It's almost winter out there and I'm inside, pacing over *the hills of my heart.*

It's late October 2020 and after my biopsies I cried over zoom to the inconsistent connection of my therapist's torso, chest, arms, and face. "The further I get away from the sexual trauma the harder it gets. I want no one to touch my body." I tell her. "The sexual trauma, the ectopic rupture pregnancy, the vestibulitis that causes painful intercourse, and now these pre-cancerous cells in my cervix each feel like a deep betrayal from my body and I will never forgive it." But later that night in my dreams I appear to myself whole. My skin is a wide open plain. Let the pack of wolves run.

Maybe it's the winter in me. There's a wolf at the door and it's me. It's me. I'm outside my own hunger. The November wind howls ever nearer. Come in. Come in. There is fuel in the belly of this beast. *I appear and disappear over the hills* of my hips, my skin. The geese above circle the park below. It's snowing on the inside, on the outside. There's a ghost in the furnace and a wolf at the door. *Let me in.*

Nothing, Killing

—*After Emily Skaja*

I wake into the stabbing of a premenstrual migraine.
And more than that, I can't stop crying at every beautiful thing.

Smoke twists off my joint, into the air around me, and I close
my eyes to the woman in illness that I have become.

Three times this year I've reapered, reaped, been reaped.
Hands gloved, I ushered a pine sisken, feathers bristled into a cardboard box.
Frantic after hours of trying to eat and discovering it couldn't swallow.

Emily Skaja writes:
"why is there nothing wild in you to explain it, nothing killing;"

I place my hand over the lid of the closed box as I speed to the Audubon
as the bird, in between long intervals of silence where I fear it has died,
flaps its wings violently and lets out a dying chirp.

They have already told me it will die.
It dies, not with my hand placed on the box.

In sleep, I dream of being fucked by someone I once knew, and I wake to
an orgasm, my body untouched; my partner in bed beside me.

Why is everything wild in me unholy, to explain it, for hours
I marvel at the weight of: ice rain pummels tree branches and
shatters them on the ground.

I race into the snow in green wool socks to the sound of screeching,
My dog has a squirrel by the tail, protruding from the small black box
that it made refuge of, and I make him drop it.

I place gloves on my hands and carry the box to the side yard.
"it's okay, it's okay, it's okay"
A large eye stares at me, squeaking, through the see-through lid.

One after the other I pry the edges open with a long flathead.

I watch as the last edge pops and the creature scampers away, hollering.

There was a time I lay down in the cab of my white ford pickup. A handful of antidepressants; when the boy I loved found me he stuck his finger down my throat until I retched.

"why / am I the chased thing
horrified to overtake myself," Emily
Skaja writes.

In December I have high-grade cell lesions scraped from my cervix
with a hot metal wire, and when I wake, I ask the nurses for my
partner, but I do not recall it.

I once tried to slice open my wrists with dull sea glass under a bridge.

Why am I the haunted thing horrified
Watching myself chase myself.

I try not to recall the paralyzed squirrel across the fence
Before the neighbor came down on it with a shovel for a merciful death.
"it's okay, it's okay, it's okay"

Bright yellow daffodils stare at me across the yard.
In middle school I walked into the garage to a deer hanging by its feet,
Stomach sliced down the middle, a cavity of pink.

For months I do not sleep.
Why is everything wild in me
killing.

After All

Mirror, mirror on the wall / I catalog my parent's house: take photos of the mugs my mom uses / as I use them / sit in the spot where she normally sits / read my book where she normally reads.

It's pandemic season / my parent's drove to Idaho to meet my new niece / I haven't spent a day in this house since summer / eight months ago / when the numbers weren't / as bad / but the stench of fear / clung to our shorts and tank tops and sunhats / like wet laundry left in the washer. I am in my mother's house / I am not my mother / my mother is not here. I pet her dogs / collect chicken eggs in her wire-mesh basket / say "Hello, goats," in her voice. Mirror, mirror / on the wall / I brush my teeth where my mom brushes her teeth / I stand in her shower / look down at my mom-like toes.

What is the difference between / where I am / what I am. I am / *being* mothered by her things.

Her quilt lays across my lap / I peek into her office / look at her storyboard on the wall / sit where she types / type where she types. Look / in the mirror / and there, my mother's most recognizable face;

I am 31 / when my mother / was 31 / I was ten / what ten-year-old daughter / isn't enamored w/ her mother's face? I blink / blink / but here / still I am / unmoored in my mother's silhouette.

I text her while inside her home / where she isn't / tell her about the woodpecker / tapping on her tin barn roof. *That's probably a flicker* / she replies / *that's how they chum in a mate.* I stand at her window / wonder if neighbors see / my shadow / believe nothing / amiss.

Mirror / mirror in the glass / I, my mother's image / trudging in her / rain boots across rainsoaked grass?

On a whim I take a left into Trillium Lake where
Mt. Hood should be reflected on the water's surface.
Once, I tell my best friend, soul mate, soul sister,
I was out here and saw an eagle swoop down
And pluck a fish right out of the water.
Rows of fishermen, the people in their kayaks,
The hikers dotting the edges yelled out and cheered,
As the eagle dipped and catapulted into the sunlight.

The mountain has gone into hiding behind a row of dusky clouds.
The air feels like it could snow in June and the bottom
Of the mountain there are glimpses of a pure white tundra.
A duck makes a beeline for us where we stand on the shore,
Dips under water and shoots back up right near our feet.
Shows off as it glides on by, holding eye contact,
Speckles glistening off the ripples.

A dead fish lays on the ground, part in the water, part out,
And who catches but doesn't release or doesn't take home,
How many of mother earth's creatures must we leave in
Purgatory when they should be free.
And why the fuck is there a plastic glove floating in the marsh grass,
What shallows shall we shallow before we come to our end.
Let the wild things be wild.

And just like that, a baker's dozen of salamanders
Meander where the water is not yet a foot deep,
Gliding around one another,
One pulls another's tail, and my best friend says,
I'd love to be one for a day,

But aren't we already what is wild and alive,
Toes pressing mud and feeling the bite
Of winter still swallowing the mountains,
Making us rope our arms around our chests,
And when I see the neon yellow fungus on a downed log
I think that's the only kind of neon sign I want to see
Flashing, *you too will come to rot on the forest floor.*
And the wild rhododendrons push out of the ground,

Peaking pink out from the trees,
But there on the ground a single shoe,
A discarded face mask, a shredded quarter of a tire.

And I want to leave everything on the side of the road,
Jeep, purse, phone, cd's,
Step into the woods with my best friend,
Two lost girls, remove our shoes and step on the crinkly,
Damp moss, forget our names, forget our names,
Turn me like an abandoned building,
Let the ivy choke our bare skinned throats.

TRUNK

at-ro-phy: *verb*

I become obsessed with a store downtown that sells taxidermy.
All day I think about the frozen fox.
Its fur stilled, unmoving.
I daydream of it coming back to life.
Lifting one dark brown paw and then another.
Lifting one dark brown paw and then another.

I keep having dreams that my legs have atrophied from lack of use.
By keep, I mean: one time.
I've thought of it repeatedly; it has become many dreams.
I crawl on my hands and knees through a hill of golden hay.
It isn't until I place my aviators on my face that I grow wings and fly.

On *Jane the Virgin,* Jane says:
"You think life is short, but I think it's long."
In an argument with my partner about the future I say:
"That's the problem. You think of life as long because yours probably will be.
But me, I think my life will be short and hard."
I have spent the last year hunkered down in our house, surviving (wasting away).

It is April 2021 and my partner adds air to my bike tires when we get home.
I let it sit out in the rain all winter long.
Moss tread on the tires, green scum on the seat.
A small degeneration of something that should be all speed.

In FEED, Tommy Pico writes:
"I would LOVE to imagine being alive in five
years but I have these bones u know?"

Each day I watch my elder dog struggle to hike up the couch.
Her back end is giving out and she pees in her sleep.
We bought her diapers, but we can't get them on her.
When we try to lift her tail, she yowls and squirms and darts away.
Each morning we wake to a trail of yellow spots down the edges of our bed.
I strip the sheets and say:
"Who is a good old lady?"

In War of the Foxes, Richard Siken writes:
"All night the trees stand silent in the dark, not touching.
I put on the deer suit. I turned my ears in all directions."
I've only ever lived in a world of deer.
First, growing up in Wyoming, then on the coast of Oregon.
Where I am in the city now, there are no deer here.
There is only the deer inside of me.
There is only me inside the deer suit, turning.

When the dream doctor arrives to examine me, I cry:
"I can't remember walking."
He shakes his head apologetically.
What is the distance between a body and an imagined body?
What is the dream between the bones?

SISTERS AND BROTHERS OF THE MOON

Last night held a bookmark / remote I called it / then laughing / remote remote remote.

Yesterday India surpassed 200,000 deaths/ newspapers say it is more/ can't keep up with the body count / they are mass cremating / seeking permission from their government to chop down more trees / keep up with the burning / demands of the bodies.

Two nights ago, full pink moon / lifted into the sky / a friend said "my moon isn't pink over here, I must have missed it" / then laughing / "it's not actually a pink moon, only the name of the April super moon" / out on the step I smoked a joint in the dark / inside I played Fleetwood Mac Sisters of the Moon / *Heavy persuasion* / *It was hard to breathe* /came inside swaying / looked up to my partner watching / a light smile.

Meanwhile / our government hoards the vaccines / could save them / a world obsessed with the bottom line / rock bottom.

"Don't you want to watch the watching dead?" / I ask and am confused by my partners look on his face / "the watching dead?" he repeats / as if we haven't been watching the death count.

They say you no longer / need / to wear a mask outside / inside w/ other vaccinated people / states lift their mandates / while mass graves are dug / head of a hospital in India says / *We have two hours of oxygen left.*

In my home alone / I yell at the dog to hush / call him my nephew's name / my little brother's name / my words aren't landing / and each millisecond someone dies / while I finish a master's degree / words drying up / what is a degree of words / you can't find the words to witness / a world filled with people, two to a hospital bed / gasping / pinned to the ground under a knee / gasping / calling for help / gasping.

I used to swim to the bottom of the local outdoor swimming pool in Wyoming / painted in the bottom corner was an octopus / "Hello, Mr. Octopus," bubbles carrying my words to the rippling surface / lime green swimsuit plastered to my tanned tummy / then press my toes down and rocket / launch from the blue / gulping in fresh mountain air.

A 31-YEAR-OLD OREGON WOMAN IS THE __th CONFIRMED CASE OF BLOOD CLOTS RELATED TO VACCINE

A week and a half after
I write a poem about a dream
About my legs atrophying
I take a walk in my neighborhood.

It's the first walk I've ever taken
In my neighborhood by myself
In the almost six years we've lived here.
I put *Jane Eyre* on audiobook.

It's not that I don't walk in my neighborhood
Because it's a bad neighborhood,
Though it's not the best,
But because there are no sidewalks and people drive 60 mph.
As if on a tear, a race for their life.

And as I walked and listened to my book
I looked at the yards, trees, flowers blooming.
I thought, yes, I could do this,
Walk in my neighborhood by myself
If I stick to the side roads and keep one headphone
Dangling so I can hear the cars' engines roaring.

It feels safe and I love to feel safe
Living in a chronically ill body
That never feels entirely safe
Or free.

I looped through streets, getting momentarily lost
Before returning home.
Drinking water, I glanced down at my leg.
A large red welt overtook
My right calf from ankle to knee.

Only 18 days prior had I gotten my vaccine,
And I knew I was in the age group and gender
Who were in a very, very small danger of
Getting a blood clot.

But I also knew that I had laid in my
Hammock for two hours that afternoon,
Devouring Lily King's *Writers and Lovers*,
So maybe a sunburn, I tried to tell myself.

But my stomach said, girl, go right now,
Get your ass to the emergency room.
So, I hopped in the jeep and waited
And the ultrasound technician said,
"I don't see a history of blood clots on your chart."

And then she didn't say another word,
But at the end, while turning off the machine,
"Your purse is so cute, oh and your shoes, they match!"
And her kindness told me everything I needed to know.

The doctor says I caught it early,
Out in the small vein on the outside of my calf,
Not traveling, only half obstructed,
And the blood thinners pulled the welt from my skin.

But even now I feel it pressing,
As if I didn't save my own life.
And the doctor said walking didn't
Cause the clot, it was already there.

And my partner said,
"Thank god you went for that walk"
And whose hand guided me out the door?
What miracle is this that I would take a walk?

And now some of you want to use
My almost death as an excuse not to do your societal duty
And get vaccinated while our country hoards vaccines
Like a toddler with its favorite shiny toys.

This isn't my first almost death
And it won't be my last, mark my words. And with
each almost death I only become more human
More walking, gaping, bleeding heart.

And thank god, who I'm not even sure I believe in,
Thank these lilacs rolling the scent of grandmothers off my breakfast bar
And thank my mom and sister who said, "It wouldn't hurt to go in and have
it checked" Even though we all chanted silently, sunburn, sunburn, sunburn.

I said to the ER doctor,
"You know, best case scenario you tell me:
Stop being a fucking idiot and put your damn sunscreen on
When your book is really good, and the hammock is calling."

And the ER doctor said,
"I'll put that in your notes,"
But then,
"Good thing you followed your intuition."

Don't let them tell you that your body isn't miracle,
That it isn't all a fizzy drink in your belly
And when it boils, get in your Jeep, blast Florence & the Machine
Belt the words and let the cars nearby see the tears stream
And don't turn to them, hands at ten and two,
And take yourself home, child.

ODE TO MY LEGS

You who have carried me carry me still,
Though last week, on the outer calf, a blood clot
At 31, and to the ER nurse I said sarcastic,
"really, 31-year-old-women getting blood clots"
And in my dreams last night the whole world was one big lake or ocean or
river,
Everywhere I looked, water
And I floated on my back, floated in a boat,
Floated on a bloated yellow ducky inflatable.
When I was 15 a boy said, "Look at them stems"
And proudly I flaunted you in my short-shorts
Years of soccer and basketball and swimming
And running, running, running:
One time two men chased me and my girl friend
At dusk, all the way back to my car
And it was you that carried me, sheer power
Force of will, slammed into the driver's side
And hit the lock button like I was cranking us up to heaven
When her bare legs hit the fabric seat next to me.
Never before have I examined my calves so much,
Slender now without the sports to tone you.
In middle school my favorite pair of jeans were stitched
Together on the outer edges by leather string.
I wore them to every school dance and when I swayed and dipped
The boys stood in a half circle, wondering how I transformed suddenly
Into such a girl.
Each time I sit on the toilet
I pull my pants down all the way to my ankles. I can't
stop examining you for obstructions under the skin,
Naked eye can't see.
I used to allow you to be hoisted above my head in the back
Of my dodge neon or bent over the top of the hood in the woods.
How am I to contend with the mechanism that holds me being something
I can't trust and when I say to my partner "going for my clot walk"
We smile, but a few days ago I read the statistics online

About the percentage of people that die within a month
After being diagnosed with deep vein thrombosis
And I started bawling and this man who doesn't cry
Welled up tears in his eyes before hugging me.
You, sinewy and wretched, used to scramble up trees to the tip top
And look down at my mom, a tiny spot below
I used to sit in the bathtub and count your bruises and scrapes
Like trophies lined on the wall of my tanned, summer-girl skin
But yesterday I sat in the shower, wanting to shave you but scared
Of the thrumming underneath the skin,
Scared of a nick that would make blood gush out
And remember when I was fifteen and I'd stretch you
To kick the soccer ball and you'd tear in the thighs
And I'd crumple on the field and be carried off by my
Dad and his best friend who'd slather icy hot
And we didn't know what was happening,
How the construction of something so solid could rip
Like a supernova.
And in my dream floating down the river road
I felt infinity, but to everyone who came near
I said, "I had a blood clot this week and now I don't trust who I am"
And when I woke, you felt numb, elevated above my heart on a stack of pillows
You felt weightless, chopped off, a body without legs to carry her home.
You, blue bird tipped dolphin tale,
Thrashing under the wake of every cerulean pool
You pumping higher and faster on the swing
Trying to reach the clouds with a tippy-toe
You blood thirsty angel wings
That gripped your younger brothers head in a headlock
Then flipped him off the bed while I didn't lose a beat
Chatting with my ninth-grade boyfriend on the cordless
You who once could crush a man
You no highway for a future child
You an empty stretch of desert road, thrumming
You stretch marked and silky-skinned
You heron stalks

You oscillating empire of grief
And fortitude and for the love of this
Good green and holy earth,
Carry me across the lands,
Please, hold me up,
Hold me planted in this sacred soil
You who have carried me, carry me still.

Blood On The Moon, Someone's Coming
—from Practical Magic

I.

At my birth, a doctor ran into the room yelling
"She has Von Willebrand! She needs plasma!"
My birth could have been an exit, my small
mother bleeding out on the table her body
unable to clot. Moon mother do not hide your
light. It is you who can raise a tidal wave
above the heads of men and wash away their
sins.

II.

Tested for the bleeding disorder,
they pricked my finger and handed me a small white disk.
Creating a blood flower to measure the flow.
Moon goddess, it is your painted ring of
blood that calls out to the stolen, lost, and
murdered woman.
This is not a crown but a protest.

III.

My sister gave birth to my nephew, an
emergency c-section.
They sliced her open, but they couldn't
staunch the flow. It's amazing she was
alive to do it again, a few years later
when my niece entered
the world the same way. Moon
mother, your rotund belly
pregnant with power.
How your revolution
Holds sway over babes and poets alike.

IV.

Blood on the moon.
Blood on the moon.
Where's my tiger's eye,
I need my tiger's eye.

V.

What does it say about us, our favorite mother-
daughter film is Practical Magic: an abusive
man gets murdered, then brought back to life,
then buried in the garden where red roses grow
from his upturned boots. And a curse on the
women promises that any man who dare love
an Owen's women will be doomed to die. But
blood is thicker than water, thicker than the
head of men who try to love you to your end.
And isn't that what we cherish about it?
Your sisters, your aunts, your mothers
know the cost and will pay it for you, to
keep you alive, again and again. Moon
goddess I work the spell of
Amas veritas, make me never fall in love.

VI.

Nineteen, I bled for forty days.
The previous four years, in love with an abusive man.
Paid a penance; Collapsed on the bathroom floor.
An ectopic rupture pregnancy,
barely any breath left in my lungs.
At the emergency room my heart rate dropped,
momentarily blipping out completely.
They wheeled me past those double white doors,
filling my body back up with someone else's blood.
Only two small pints of what remains, my own.
blood is not transactional:
your blood, my blood, our blood.
Moon mother, you have watched me as I've slept,
as I've dreamt, as I've fucked under the trees.
You are lantern, your ring of sorrow will guide me home.

VII.

At Beck Lake in Wyoming
trailing behind our mom.
She stopped to cut cattails with her
pocketknife, nicked her finger and for two
miles we walked to the parking lot, her
hand lifted in the air, blood dripping down
her arm. I stared at the hot summer asphalt,
following the blood stains of my mother.
Moon goddess, wherever we are, be it under
California, Wyoming, Texas, or Oregon
skies, there you are, above. You watch with
me, the trails of my mother.
You sat, milky in the daylight sky
saw my moon mother crumpled near
the mother hens in her garden, the
day her mother died.

VIII.

At the ER I tell the doctor that
I think there is a blood clot
underneath the welt of red skin
on my leg.
Where blood is supposed to flow it is no
longer. If this is a plague then why has
my river run dry, is it not supposed to
run red with blood?
Moon mother, just three days prior I
sat on the stoop in the dark, watched
you rise orange and magnetic over the
towering cedars, came into the house
dancing, grateful to be alive.

IX.

I cover my body in red clay mud from the desert, paint
my nails crimson, spit cherry pits, one by one, back
into a glass bowl. I cut back the red roses that tower
above my head, thinking about the man I might have
buried under there, if given half the chance. Moon
goddess, in a few days you will be a Blood Moon
hanging over the sky and I'll dance to Stevie Nicks
thinking about my recent beach trip with my sister
and mom where we twirled around the living
room, cold sober and feral.

X.

There's blood on the moon, blood in my veins
that isn't mine. The rivers ran red with the
blood of my mother,
of my sister, of me.
Each month I bleed, a cost I
don't calculate. The men
I love are doomed to die.
There's *blood on the moon,*
Moon mother, moon goddess,
I pray to you, show them
what we are made of.
They try to drown us, but we
are tidal, eclipse, revolution.

HEART ROT

Prunus Serrulata

And after all this time, I
am still not sure where
my heart lies when I go
to sleep.

When the cherry blossom began
to hollow out, to fill its crevices
with cobwebs, with tiny white
mushrooms, was it preparing
for death?

And when lady *laetipous sulphureus*
flourished, opened her
fan of yellow and orange
lace at the center of the
tree, did it know what it
suffered from?

Did it feel the sickness
in its waxy leaves, its
pastel pink petals, its
plundering roots?

Did it know that we all
suffer from
heart sickness,
from hollow
hearts disease?

Will we ever know our hearts? Know them the
way a tree knows every groove of the bark on
its body. Or what it feels like to be a home for
the birds.

Sweet tree, are you ready to die?
When your tears echo, they
sound a lot like mine.

What Happened to The Body is Not a Poem

What they don't tell you is that your body, in response to trauma, can make its own rules and manifest pain where there should be pleasure.

While watching the movie *Moxie*, a girl speaks in front of a crowd of other girls: my boyfriend raped me in my own bed, in my own room. And there's something about that sentence, that word, that awakens in me a formidable shock wave. I am thrashed by it. All these years, twelve years since I was with the boyfriend who did what the girl on the movie said he did but in all sorts of other places, like my car, like beds at friend's houses, and all these years I've called it *sex*. Called it *fucking*. Called it everything but what it was when it turned violent, when it turned forceful, and I cried cause I wanted it to stop but it didn't stop. He wouldn't stop. And even now I won't type the word, I'll type it, but not in reference to me. Not as something my body endured.

What they don't tell you is that your body, in response to trauma, can find itself more closed up, closed off, *Sorry, we're not open and may never open again*, years after the trauma takes place, than it was in those first few months or years.

After 413 days without, I nudge my partner toward the bedroom after he comes out of the bathroom. We've been together nine and a half years now. *Have sex with me*, I say, a churning that has been resting in my belly for months now but which I haven't been able to verbalize or make a move toward or acquiesce. He rushes to the room and immediately strips bare, and I say, *Jesus, calm down*. Calm down. The pain comes, sharp and hot like I'm being torn in two, but shortly it is replaced by pleasure and then exhaustion.

What they don't tell you is that your body, in response to sexual assault, can produce a painful condition in which the vagina responds to penetration as if it were an enemy, an invader, and the opening swells, red-hot and wound-up, wounded.

If you don't treat a traumatic instance or reoccurrence like a wound, it will become one on its own. When you say *psychosomatic* what people think you mean is, it's all in your head, but what started in the body went to the head and the head spit it out, back into the body, so the trauma you felt in an instance(s) is replicated, as if you never stop being assaulted in the back seat of your Dodge Neon, in a bed, in your home.

What they don't tell you is that the body, in response to trauma, will try to turn that trauma into a lovely poem, but what happened is not a poem. It will try and talk about the trees towering overhead where the car was parked, about the pressure of a hand you loved clasped over your mouth in a shhhh, shhhh, shhhhh, of silence. It will write it out and out and out, a million different ways. It will still be trying to write it.

We All Got Burnt

> "i did not lose someone i love. i lost someone i once loved."
> —Olivia Gatwood

I can curl my body up.

I can park a dead boy down, right
there on the poem.
Because I've got dead boys too.

One
Two

My dead boys are just like your dead boys.
One I didn't love but thought about it, a
time or two.
The other, well, I loved with childlike wonder.

In middle school at the skatepark
He tried to kiss me on the lips.
I turned my face and gave him the cheek.

I've got dead boys that aren't dead boys too.

Three
Four

The one that gripped my breasts while we kissed,
Like doorknobs, like fistfuls of grass,
Something he wanted to pull out.
Leaving putrid yellow bruises that
Battered my pale skin for weeks.

The one that had half a front tooth
Knocked clean out, then got drunk, then kissed me on the
floor of my friend's room.
He wanted to love me but, girl, I would never.

Five
Six

The one that kissed me when he
wanted to kiss another.
The one I kissed when I wanted to
kiss another.

Seven
Seventy
Seven Hundred and Seventy-Seven.

The one I loved. The one I loved. The one I loved.
He's the deadest of them all.
Gatwood writes:
"I want to know what it
means to survive
something.
/
does it just mean
I get to keep my body?"

The one that said, "Where did you learn those moves?"
The one that cut my labia with a jagged nail, then
punched and spidered my windshield with his fist
cause I could no longer fuck.
The one that knew how to kiss so as to buckle my knees.
The one that said, "No matter where you go, I'll find you."
The one that held his hand over my mouth. The one that I hid
from in a ditch with a pocket-knife while he drove up and
down the black and rainy logging roads and called my name
and screamed my name and cried it.
The one who wept, "I'm sorry, I'm sorry, I'm sorry." The
one who left fingerprints on my skin.

Eight
Nine
Ten
Eleven

The one who stole me from my abusive lover
(thought he was saving me)
Who wanted to be choked, be hit. And I
cried while we kissed, closed my eyes to
the face that wasn't his.

The one I didn't love who
tilted my chin up gently.
The one I didn't love who
loved another.
The one I was with just to feel.
The one who loved me when I
loved another.
The one who loved me when I loved another.
The one who loved me when I loved another.

Ring around the rosie,
A pocket full of dead boys.
Ashes, ashes.
"On your knees," they said.
Down, down, go down.

So You Wanna Talk About How I'm The Dead Girl

1.

I'm not saying I'm Ophelia floating in the water before she drowns, but lately when I try to fall asleep, I can't catch my breath, like Hamlet's hands are holding me underwater, my legs tangled in ragweed, seaweed, there's lost souls under the River Styx and they think I'm ready to join them. I won't go under into the dreamy place where flowers will float me on down the stream, and it isn't until I swallow a tablet of Ativan that I'm the river and the sky and Ophelia singing before she died. They say: forgive him, he knows not what he does, but I've got forgiveness for no man, no jesus up in the clouds, only the heron that sits on the riverbank, watching me drown, her keen yellow eye silent, unjudging, waiting to deliver me.

2.

When I was a child, a young girl my age a town over was
found chopped up and left in a dumpster, her scooter intact
beside her. Before that I climbed on top of the dumpster in our
neighborhood so I could see over the rim of the trailer park to
a field where horses roamed. After that, I became afraid of
dumpsters and what lurked inside them, learned that people
out there thought girl's bodies were yesterday's trash. When
grown men drove by my 12-year-old body, craned their necks,
honked their horns, I flipped them off. Fuck if I'm going to
become another casualty of my female body, I thought, as if a
mere finger could stave off their gnawing hunger. But then I fell
in love with a boy who became obsessed with extinguishing my
light. It burnt brighter than his own, his already yesterday's cig
ashes blown away in the wind. And when I hid from him on a
rainy night in a ditch, pocketknife curled into my cold hand, I
became the girl in the dumpster and realized I had been her all along.

3.

There's a market for dead girls. It's bigger and wider
than you could even fathom. When you Google dead
girl paintings there are hundreds of listings. Under Fine
Art America it says, "Choose your favorite dead girl
paintings from 695 available designs." I don't want to
be your favorite dead girl. I don't want my head stuffed
and mounted on your wall, glassy eyeballs following your
every move across your room. I won't go walking after
dark and if I do, I'm taking my 75-pound pit bull. He's kind
and scared of everyone, especially men, but you don't need
to know that; you just need to imagine his jaw the size of
your face closing around it. And when you hear his bellow
it's my rally cries you're hearing, for all the dead girl paintings
plastered on the museum walls. We are a veritable field of
wildflowers, on our backs, singing and floating down
a stream, our bodies brush strokes before we're dead.

The Mouth of the River

Three days of bleeding is no big deal except when you know that you're dying. Scratch that. Feel that you're dying. But it's only been three days and four biopsies ago and the phone hasn't rung because, "closer to 7 days," they said when they were *violating* you on the table, but they don't call it violating they call it medical procedure that you signed off on after they shoved lidocaine cotton balls up your yoo-hoo and you pushed up the table and away. They call it a bed, but you know better, it's a table and it might as well be stainless steel and they might as well be pulling your body naked and frigid out of a cooler with the other bodies.

And your sister made you a grilled turkey and cheese sandwich afterwards that she also made for her kids like you're a kid who needs taken care of because you are because you might have cervical cancer. You've been sick for 15 years and you're only 30 but it sometimes feels like 68.

The doctor says, you'll feel a pinch. She says it after the pinch. "I'm going to hurt you," they say after already hurting you. Why can't anyone be upfront about the way bodies betray. Not just my own, but also yours and yours and yours and yours and the first boy I loved who tore me apart.

The doctor says the vestibulitis (vaginal pain) might be caused from sexual trauma and I don't say a word but when they've got the speculum up there and they're taking samples of my body from my body I breathe like I'm in labor. But that can't be right because labor is something people do that gives them babies but when I was twenty a fallopian tube exploded, and I almost died and since then labor isn't something I do. What I do is sit on the couch and think about dying and watch the birds and I don't have sex because it hurts so bad, but I think about having sex as if sex is something I can do.

I tell me partner while driving in the car about the procedure and how the doctor says the pain is in the opening of me, the mouth of the river, and it might be caused because of what someone I loved did to me repeatedly which is to say: he'd be high and he'd fuck me for hours and hours because he couldn't get off and I'd be dry and I'd be swollen and I'd be crying and I'd be so exhausted I couldn't hold my body weight up anymore and he'd eventually pull out and shove my body over like a piece of trash, like it's my body's fault that his body wouldn't let him and then eventually when he'd calm down we'd start again and I'd try not to cry out in pain and try to let my body absorb his body. And my partner listens to me say, "it might be caused from sexual trauma," though I don't elaborate and then he begins telling me about a guy who was driving like a psycho and cut around him in the bike lane to get in front of him and then slammed on his breaks. And he's not telling me like it's a comparison but because he's uncomfortable with what I'm telling him and grown men who don't abuse woman's bodies can't think, let alone talk about the abuse of women's bodies. And while he's telling me this, I'm thinking about that boy I loved who used to follow me home, wait in the baseball field below my house 'til everyone was gone, without me knowing. How a friend said, "I used to chase homeboy out of the field in the middle of the night while he was stalking you."

And I think about being on that table. But you can't say this to anyone. In bed I tell my partner "I wish I could talk to you about this stuff" and he says "talk" And we lay there in silence until I eventually hear his light snoring. And I'm back on the table and the doctor says, "Because of the significant cell growth we're most likely going to have to do the LEEP procedure and because you don't tolerate this well, we will put you under and do it in surgery."

LEAP, and I think I'm a frog and I think I can just jump off the table, off the bed, hop on out of here when it's done. Hop, hop, hop. And my mom said, says, said, "When I was 32, they did the LEEP without any anesthetics or pain meds or lidocaine, right there in the GYNO's office because it was the 90's and Wyoming. And then I went to the grocery store and to a BBQ and to your brother's baseball game and then white-water rafting and then I hemorrhaged."

"Just a pinch," the doctor says. I check for hemorrhaging. But I think the blood is like tears and the ones that I haven't cried and the ones that I have, and the tears might go on forever, because it's the mouth of the river down there and the rivers ran red with blood and the ocean could be dying, might be dying. I swear I read something about coral reefs, but each time I think about it I feel myself again, on that table, and she keeps trying to pull the speculum out: "Every time I move it a little you start gushing again" And I think, *no surprise,* but I don't say a word because I keep doing my labor breaths like the movies taught me.

I'm trying to visualize myself by a river, but I am the river and eventually I turned from *you*, as if this poem were about anyone but me. I wanted to disassociate, to shove it away, and it was you on the table but now it's me even though I'm at home on the couch and she pulls it out and I close my legs under the sheet ghost of a cover they gave me. Silent tears stream down my face.

But is it from the possibility of cancer? Or the violation? Or the realization that someone I loved did me so dirty, which I already knew, fucked me so wrong, that now everything near the mouth is a violation and when I say mouth I mean vagina. I mean opening. I mean place where a baby will never come from and that part isn't his fault it's my body's fault, but it feels a little bit like a sick joke that someone played on me.

"Do you want a tissue?" she holds out a box "For my eyes or my vagina?" I laugh, but it's dark and she sees it's dark even though the florescent lights beat down. "For both," she says, "for both." And then she leaves the room. My butt is naked on the table-bed and the silent tears become full raking sobs and I don't even know what I'm crying about but two minutes later when I dress and open the office door, and the nurse aid who was in the room hearing me labor breathe looks at me, must have heard me bawling through the wall, with such knowing that sitting here thinking about it could make a grown woman cry. "How do I get out of here?" I whisper, and she points to an exit sign, but I still feel turned around, upside down, down, down, down, scoot your butt down to the end of the table please.

And now my tea is cold and it's still about four days 'til the phone will be ringing, and I'm still bleeding but I know what they will say, just like I knew when I was waiting for the phone call from the pap that came a week later when I was in a vintage clothing store and the doctor said, "high grade cell lesions" and I nodded along, yes yes, like I knew all along. There's a procedure in my future, but when I'm there it doesn't feel like a violation it feels like an empty dream. We could all use an empty dream. And when I wake up, I'll say something like, "My body is a real fun home" Like I told the doctor at the pap where she found the cell lesions when I lay splayed on the table like I am the mouth of the Columbia River.

I am the mouth.

But I don't tell you this. I don't tell any of you this. I say, "I might have cancer, but it's fine. I'm okay, everything is okay." I'm watching a squirrel eat a fallen apple from the apple tree in a pile of leaves and there's a black-capped chickadee at the bird feeder and I'm ghosting my trauma even as December nears and the heater is blasting a quiet humming song.

Unraveled Me

I keep thinking about this sweater dress I wore in high school.
The knit fabric stretched and separated,
Exposed diamond constellations of skin.
I felt in it the yearning of the whole world,
Not mine, though mine was a dried-out bale of hay
Such thirst.

For as long as I can remember I wanted to collect
The yearning of others.
I felt it in the power of my hips, swinging.

It's about control, you see. Power.

Now, I control where the cups and plates go in the cupboards.
What we watch on tv every night, the remote near my hand.
I decide what and when we will eat, though really,
All my medications that I time around food decide that for me.
I'm the one who structures the world in tiny boxes around me.

I think of the boys who loved me,
How there is no hometown house to return to.
No one yearns for the sick girl,
And if they do, they are only yearning for the
Remembered version of my sweater dress,
Cut-off shorts, muscled calves,
I want her too. I'd crawl on my knees,
Bow down to the heatwave,
Just to fuck her in the forest one more time,
Out by the waterfall, see me that way.

I can't imagine what she would think of me,
All tired eyes and loose ends.
It's not that I've come undone it's that
I've been undone before, pulled the thread on

That sweater dress and let the diamonds hit the floor,
And when you've been made of crystalline forces—

What's left when you no longer love your body:

An untrustworthy writhing thing who will lead you astray,
No not down that trail in the woods,
But here, to the hospital, to the ER
Drink up blood suckers and by blood suckers
I mean the IV's dangling from my arm.

I know you don't want to hear this,
But I spend all my time dreaming about love,
About making love,
About kissing women I don't know,
About kissing boys I've loved,
About kissing, kissing, kissing.
Every inch of my—but
This body, touched in violence,
In illness, in trepidation—won't allow you,
All you, forked tongues,
The devil is in me, it's in you.
I want to be a serpent,
But I'm just a spool of blood-red
Thread, unwinding.

I want to meet me again.
But this new me is all turbulence
And not the fun kind.
No running through the trees,
No floating down the river,
No hooded eyes and long looks,
Just a panic attack at the tea house
And masking my desire with rage.

I still step in the grass in my bare feet,
After years of coloring, I'm letting my blond
Hair grow in, only to discover it dirty dishwater blond,
Like all the lightning in my storm has been wrung out.
I'm trying to let the roots tangle over the empty house.
I still want to be Gillian from *Practical Magic*,
Be the dark horse, dream of smoking cigarettes in my sleep,
Cut my hands open, cut my heart open,
Let the bad men come to me,
Let the wind stir up all my old haunts,
Feel your eyes on me, pretend I can't see you
Let the world see it on paper,
Watch me, untethered sweater,
Unraveling in the dark.

BRANCHES

Mistress Winter

I'm waiting for the sheets of ice
to cover the ground, for the icicles
to drip from the picnic table,
the power pole, the mailboxes, and
trees that line the street.
The ice will be so biting
that trees over fifty-years-old
will tear out their roots
just to shatter the pieces on the ground.
There will be floods racing
to see who can be the first to
drown out the rest of us.
When the waters rage and the
rain pours for days on end,
will we finally learn how to cry?
We need winter this year;
The hollow gutting out of the land,
the stripped trees, the tower of blankets
as we huddle into our own darkness.
Our emptiness tight from all the sweating.
We don't need a gentle cleanse
but a rough and raging detox.
We need the winds to whip through the land,
the plants to bow to its glory.
The whisper as it puts us to sleep.

It's March   Again

I see the backyard neighbor,
          blond hair bobbing near the metal fence   line.

We seek separation, but there she is
                              on the border   weaving   looping
     wisteria vines into my side of the fence.

A day later   there I am.   blond hair
bobbing near the metal fence   line.
               I thread   the   vine.   Tug.   Thread.

The vines weave themselves around one another, binding.
          They grab hold the dying lilac   they're choking
                    the hollow   trunk,   but no gasps.

Only the wind   sighs.

I see myself   the other side of the fence.
          Blond hair   bobbing.

A wisteria tapestry.   ·Soon periwinkle buds
          will curtain the mirror.

It's March   again,   and I stare out at the world from across a room.

Duck, Duck, Goose

When the abled-anti-maskers say,
"Only those with preexisting conditions,"
I turn away from uncles, aunts, childhood schoolmates.
F for friend. F for family.
F for Fuck you.

I tip-toe barefoot through grass and moss,
Damp from light mist.
Carry book, letter, heart lantern.
Preexist in my pea green hammock.
Preexist cradled, held, swinging.

I list the ways they tell me,
Faces uncovered,
Groups at the beach, at bars, at the corner of:
Give me a haircut and my body my choice,
Like a mask is the vagina, the tubal ligation
They refused me at 20,
after my heart stopped twice from ectopic rupture.
At 25, the "you might change your mind,
Might want to try to die to birth."
At 30 now, left waiting.
Say sick is not whole.
Sick is un-mattered,
Unmothered, Un-abled.
A preexisting ghost.
In Japan they told rollercoaster riders,
Please scream inside your hearts.

I hold my breath when I pass someone
Unmasked, unbothered.

I will not be your goose.

Hold my breath on the street,
Next to my partner while he sleeps.
Hold, hold,

Still holding.

As if I'm trying to take my death
Into my preexisting hands.

Swaying in the hammock.
Blink into the fractured light
Scream into the dying cherry blossom.

I don't listen to the betrayals
Of the body.
Don't hear them say,
"Dead, dead, dying."

A hand on my head
Is my neighbor
Is my friend
Is my lover.

And Anyway / And Never Mind

The kind of people who say / write EVERY day / aren't my kind of people / aren't spending two hours in the sun only to wake / your right brain in a vice / kind of people / did the dishes and your neck went stiff / chronic migraine kind of people / have to restrict their diet / still get sick / kind of people / three stomach disorders / afraid to be far away from their toilet / kind of people / chronically fatigued / chronically ill / chronically I'm sick of all your shit / kind of people.

And anyway / you can be rejected by journals and presses / every day / they can tell you / your work is / "full-throated, textured, out loud singing" / yet still dump you in the rejection bin / but have you ever / asked your thirteen-year-old-nephew / if he wanted to go swimming at the river with you / and he said no / for the first time / no longer the cool aunt / no longer happy to ride shotgun in your jeep / get gutted like that, my friends / fillet that fish / fry me up / I'll take / "best of luck placing this" / or "your writing is not for us" / over realizing that I'll be almost 50 / if I make it that far / by the time my nephew wants to hang out with me again.

And never mind / that when I did go to the river / niece in tow / still not yet old enough to reject me / we saw a crawdad / hawk dining on the opposite bank / mama and papa geese / two ends of a line / and the mountain water froze the blood in our bodies / my leg where there is a blood clot / throbbed / but I floated / and the two pings of email rejections I got while there / floated by / nothing like dreams matter / when my kind of people / all around me on pool noodles / effervescent / watching the crows flit over / from our bellies or our backs.

And I can't tell you / the horror that ricocheted / when my elder dog fell from the bed in her sleep / and when I touched her belly she didn't move / felt like she didn't breathe / and I yelled at my partner / "Roxy is dead! She's dead!" / but then, I flicked on the lamp / heart hammering / and she blinked her eyes / dazed on the floor wondering how she got there / my kind of people / how did we get from such great heights / back into the dirt.

So let me tell you / writers / bleeders / no / I won't follow your antiquated ideas / of creation / I must pet this dog / and remember my nephew's hugs / for surely soon those will stop too / and howl at the moon / when it rises in the sky / and nurse this rhododendron back to health / much like my body / too much sun / your dying / too much water / your dead / I must go to the bathroom thirty times today / nurse my head with an ice pack / call upon my old gods and new / turn circles / high step it out of here to make the blood flow.

My kind of people / blow bubbles / with their pool noodle / under the river water / examine a crawdad with a missing leg / scream and run from the river / yelling / today is not the day they will be eaten by a large salmon / laugh when they want to cry.

Everywhere I Look Things Keep Dying

Watched a hummingbird flit to the fuchsia and collect dreams on the tip of its beak.

Watched its iridescent green feathers sparkle in the fire season sunlight.

Heard my young dogs voice go hoarse from barking.

Watched my old dog age slow, slowly, slower now.

Woke from a prophetic dream.

Someone telling me I don't have much time left with her and to enjoy it.

Watched a fly land on her head and go unnoticed.

Watched her corn cob the edge of the bed, her sleep routine.

Watched my stoic partner wrap her in a hug.

Tried not to imagine our collective heartbreak at what is around the corner.

Tried not to cry at the remembering of what will pass.

Felt the warm slime of the ultrasound on my leg.

Closed my eyes as the technician checked for the reminisce of my blood clot.

Heard him say "what was there before is not there."

Saw the rat, belly up in the rat trap my partner set.

Its head squished between the jaws.

Wished for a tiny Viking boat to send it down a creek and light it on fire.

Saw a woman come into the movie theater for the first time in a year and a half and start crying.

Handed her napkins.

Told her not to worry, the movie she was going into would give her ample weeping material.

Watched a group of molting crows dip their breadcrumbs and plums into my bird bath.

Got called to the door by my partner to see a hawk standing rigid in the bird bath.

Watched him cooling his claws.

Saw the hawk swoop through the branches of the trees and away.

Laughed when my partner said, "I think it's the same hawk I saw chasing a cat a few years ago".

As if there could only be one almighty predator per neighborhood.

As if I wasn't one, stalking the daylight at each turn.

This sunflower

Ornate mustard yellow head dangling /

That's what the honeybees thought of me
All those years,
White, blond hair, glistening like pollen

But now / when the colors have all gone

What's left: extra cotton shoved behind my ears
Into the la, la, la
Of it all
Trying to extinguish, burnt petals while they are still living

That's what disease is like, and by disease, I mean you, what you did to me still
lingers
And also / what my body does, did, will do to me, it's
Extraterrestrial

How one minute I'm watching a sunflower die, the next, I watch you pop
The heads off the dandelions
One by one by one,
And it still rings in my ear, when I hear you say,
"You're like an innocent flower"
And there you are, repeated, still hell / bent on destruction of beautiful things,
A series of misgiving that you lent me, a haunting that I can't outrun, can't
shake,
Think I want to until the
D I E ease of it all forgets me.

SKY

Bird Burden

A crow has been calling in the front yard since the sun rose. It's the beginning of November and my left breast feels heavy. I lift it and the pressure does not release. I think it must be my heart weighted, hiding under and masking itself as my breast. So heavy that it's pressing through flesh. It will fall out or erupt through my thorax. I try to redistribute my weight to no avail. My right breast feels empty in comparison, but the pressure on the left is so immense that I feel a tug on my clavicle.

When the crow stops calling the sounds of the world become unbearable. The heater trundles. The recycling truck barrels down the street, a thousand-pound monster that clutches and crushes the glass in its teeth. I hear cars zooming at a distance.

Yesterday my partner cooked a turkey that had been in the freezer since last November. I ate from the right side of the turkey's breast, so what I'm feeling has no mathematical logic.

Yesterday, a sick pine siskin appeared on my back patio under the bird feeder. I watched the bird for over two hours. It would try and eat but the food would fall from its mouth. It slept, small beak nestled into the dark stripes of its feathers, right in the center of the top stair. My dogs stared at it hungrily and six lesser goldfinch landed on the step, collecting birdseed around it, mere inches away, while the sick bird slept, before I finally got a call from the wildlife care center telling me what was going on. The Portland Audubon Society says there is an outbreak of salmonella. I brought in my feeders, sprayed down the patio. I placed gloves on my hands, took a cardboard box, and cornered the poor bird. It tried to flap its wings, but it couldn't fly. It hopped and dodged. Eventually, I laid my hand flat in front of it. It stepped on to my finger and I placed it quietly on the towel in the box. On the 40-minute drive to the wildlife care center I placed my hand atop the box. "Shhhh," I said, "Shhhh. It will be okay." The birds keep alighting on the tree near where the feeder used to be.

There are birds on my skin: a crow on my right thigh reading a stack of books in a river, a dove flying under a quote about sharing burdens, a girl releases a small bird on my arm. Next week I'll add a heron standing in the marshes of my hometown. The heron in his oversized grey coat. The heron stalking.

I awoke in a panic to the pressure in my left breast. There was a moment I was sure that the precancerous cells in my womb have confused my body, claiming it as a hospitable environment for the lesions and given them a pathway, a trail, a direct route to follow to reach my breast.

I think my breast is turning into a wing. Or they become wings at night as I sleep, and I only turn back into a woman as I wake. It is getting more difficult for my bird to make this transition every night.

When I was 17 or 18, I took mushrooms one winter night and drove home in the darkest night I'll ever see. Around my room I busied myself, trying to outrun the fear that dogged me. I stood in front of the long doors of my closet that stretched out like teeth. Over and over, I changed my clothes, as if I could change who and what I was. A disguise. As I pulled my shirt over my head I looked down and saw my breasts pull from my body, extend out to the side, an extra set of elbows. This image still haunts me some days when I look down while changing. But now, looking back, I think they might have been wings not elbows. I was preparing for flight.

I've been trying to fly away from my own body for at least 13 years. Maybe longer. I've been sick since the winter I was born. Maybe if I had been born what I am—a bird, a bird—then I wouldn't feel the weight of my left breast bogged down by my heart and I could fly up into the sky and scream.

For 370 Days

I kneel on the floor and tell my partner's mom

> Doing puzzles
> > Is the only thing
> > > That shuts my mind off.

When my lips are dry and I press them together.
I open my mouth lightly, not enough for my lips to part.
Stuck together, there is a light tug:
Pink parchment sewn together.

> > > > > A violent hush.

Bustling Bazaar teal nail polish shines from my fingers.

> I piece and piece and piece a puzzle.
> > "I like the way I put a puzzle together, admire it,
> > > And then I get to tear it up, destroy it, and put it back in the box."

A squirrel sits on the handle of an axe jutting out from a stump.
The dogs bark mad circles at the sliding back door.
I yank the blackout curtains wide open:
Let the blinding teeth of light in.

> > > > > A silent hum.

Each letter on the FANFUCKINTASTIC puzzle is a Crayola color.

> I pack petunias into pots, spaced equally apart.
> > I stack color-coded books on my shelf like tetris.
> > > I always do the frame first, then stare into the mouth of the puzzle.

The hammock sways under the force of my right foot, rocking it.
A rose finch couple lands in a tree near its nest, swiveling heads.
They each have chunks of grass and twigs in their beaks.
They set to weaving the pieces of their nest under the bough of the shed.

A twittering tapestry.
Which is puzzle.
Which is trombone.
Which is home.

Bird Shit At Dusk

In Italy it is supposed to be good luck or a good sign when a bird shits on you. When
I was a child in the heat of Wyoming summers, we would set up a tent

in the side yard of our trailer and camp out under the fathomless western sky.
On the few nights my mom wasn't working, trying to provide for three children

on her own, she would read to us, and on one such camp-yard night we laid in the
grass, poking out from the jaws of the tent opening. A flock of birds flew

overhead and I turned my face of childhood wonder toward the clouds at which point
one of the flock released a cannon ball of shit into my eye and on to my

Precious Moments bible. By then I was already questioning God about his existence.
Was he a dream that someone else had concocted? Was I a dream inside someone's

mind, but if so, who was it that dreamt of me and how were they created? Now, at 31
I've nearly died more times than one, and in the dark of death I haven't seen a single thing

I lay in the hammock near the bird feeders and watch their shadows flit above my languid
body. Every time one flies above, I think, *please don't shit on me.* But when they

pass by without blunder, I wonder if my luck passed, if I never had any to begin with.
Maybe the birds won't shit on me because god is just a word and the only holy thing left

in me is this desire to be blessed, anointed, baptized by bird shit falling from the sky, as if
tiny feathery angels make the judgment calls about who lives and who will die.

A Brief History
—After Billy-Ray Belcourt

Sitting in a sapphire blue camp chair under the
cherry blossom reading:
A History of My Brief Body by Billy-Ray Belcourt:
"A tree screams in the forest—forgive me,
not a tree, but an explosion of girls, an
apocalypse of girls."

Just then a violent altercation takes place
in the air from my bird feeder to the tree,
and in the cacophony of bird screams
I look up to see an Old World Sparrow
attacking a female Rose finch
whom weaves her nest of green
on the lip of the shed roof.
All around them pink petals rupture
from the flowers in the fight.
A Black Capped Chickadee rushes over,
protecting the Rose Finch.
The Old World Sparrow and the Rose Finch
collide and hit the ground at the base of the trunk.
My dog rushes over, breaks up the fight
and the birds take off, resuming their fight
in the air toward the plum tree in the neighbor's yard.
Their explosion of screams
reverberates to my bare toes.
Heart pounding, I usher myself
to the back of the yard and stand on my tiptoes,
searching for the source of the sounds.
"We don't have bird fights here!" I call,
like I can usurp the Old World order.
In my mind, a pacing.
I feel myself on this earth, a wrecking ball.

By the time I sit back down with the book
I am ravenous.
"I eat and eat until I'm more dandelion than anything else."
My dog walks over and kisses me. I turn to his dinosaur
eyes and share a thought whose lineage
can and can't be traced.
This is a New World Order.

Is there sorrow in the sparrow when the singing is done?

Moon Landing

Last night a grown man with wings appeared in
my snowy backyard. He pulled a giant white
hare down from the sky, but found he could not
swallow it.
He came to the back door where I waited.
"I'm so hungry," he said.
I'd seen this starving sickness before in the pine sisken.
Hush, hush. It's okay.
I fed him cranberries from my outstretched hand.
He took them in the beak that he didn't have.

I sent him next door where I knew the
woman would be making bird soup.
And what a good story, I thought.

When the moon is out, I
step outside.
I call to my partner,
"Look at the moon! Look at the moon!" He
barely turns his head.
"Yep, it's a moon," he says.

I thought, what a good dream. But
when I woke there was a bird body in
the cup of my hands.
I can't see it, but there, the ruffled feathers:
there, the kind body of a hungry man.

I left the hare in the yard, a lump of
fur and snow-soaked blood.
There's a full moon on tonight.

My partner turns his back to me, bends
when I am bending.
"Moon landing," he giggles, a
line from Modern Family.
"We is butt to butt," he says. But when I
dream of the bird man, it's him whose
wings are too small, who I cannot nourish,
who I dare not touch.

Ode to Lost Things

This isn't about the cozy soccer tournament sweatshirt that I lost sometime after the fourth grade, though it is also a letter to that sweater. It's not a box of things disappeared, though it is also a box and inside the box there is a heart and the heart is inside a body and the body is and isn't mine. She used to be, but now she's her own, she's separate and she's lonely and I will spend the day curating sadness to give her somewhere to place her feels.

Ode to my pumping, climbing crawling, kicking, bruising, burnt, and benevolent thighs. Ode to the gap in them that has cradled the heads of boys, the heads of men, the heads of boys who thought they were men and thought the power of men lay in the control and seizure of women's bodies. Goodbye to reaching my toes and past them. Goodbye to the trees I used to climb, the fields I used to run, my muddied shoes, my wild blond hair flowing out behind me. It isn't enough that I wore my childhood best friend's white Pooh Bear tennis shoes into the mud-soaked field next door and ruined them, getting us both in trouble with her mother, but that those shoes have been dumped in some trash bin somewhere along the way and I can't ever lace them up again.

This isn't a love letter to my body, though every time I search for that hatred of what she was, what she has become, I think about climbing to the top of the dumpster in our trailer park and looking toward the horses roaming in the dusky fog out yonder. I rebuild mud castles, frog ponds, wreck my brand-new bicycle, pink and purple polka dot siding, in the neighbor's gravel driveway, marvel later in the bathtub at the cuts and scrapes and bruises, count them like trophies I mount on my walls.

Remember the way she used to hike mountains? Remember running down a mountain, cigarette glowing, embers red in the darkness, laughing until my sides hurt, rolling down frog hill at the frog park, unafraid of spiders or dog poop or what lay down there at the bottom of the fall. I dream about jumping off the rocks of waterfalls, of catapulting into the Shoshone River, get kicked up and swifted by the current around the bank where my dad waited to grab my life jacket and tow me in.

Ode to howling at the moon like a wolf. Ode to being a wolf, that hunger in me still. Ode to firepits and fireworks, fucking and fighting and frenching in the backseat of my dodge neon. Ode to love to love to love, the thing we all must lose in the end, the thing that is lost only to be found new and whole again, to be found empty and wanting, to be left, to be reasoned with, to be justified, to be dismantled, to be, to be, to not be.

Ode to the belly flops and the battles and the bloody noses. Farewell to soccer balls and cleats and bathing suits and hiking boots and basketball hoops and jammed fingers taped together, stinky sweaty socks, and the taste of ice blue Gatorade on the side of a grassy field. Farewell to jump rope and horseback and oranges, grapes, apples, lasagna, spaghetti, cheesecake, corn syrup, Marlboro reds and margaritas, and all the other fucking worldly delights I cannot taste again.

Hello to dreams. Hello to migraines and back braces and chiropractors and rheumatologists and metal wires heated to scrape out cancerous cells. Hello to night terrors and small love, and death to passion and sex and skinny dipping and fucking in fields and running, running, running. Hello diarrhea, my old friend, I think that's how the song goes, and fuck you to doctors and hospitals and blood clots and dying, dying, chronic illness the slowest dying there ever was. Ode to tears I do not cry and ode to rage, my old friend, maybe that's how the song really goes. That's it, that's the love song, hello anger ye old bitch, remember that dead dog you watched slowly decompose in a ditch.

Ode to lovers, ode to, god damnit, I can't do it anymore, ode to she-who-must-not-be-named, which is she, which is my body, which is and isn't the villain all along. Ode to my tiny perceived losses, stacked up like the books on my numerous shelves, the only way I know how to live now. Ode to loving her. Ode to remembering her. Ode to this epitaph: She used to be something to see.

Acknowledgements

at-ro-phy:verb first appeared in *Pork Belly Press*'s zine: *Love Me, Love My Belly*

Prunus Serrulata first appeared in the *M Review* (now defunct)

The Mouth of the River first appeared in *Malasana*

Mistress Winter and After All first appeared in the *Clackamas Literary Review*

Bird Burden first appeared in *Entropy*

Nothing Killing, We All Got Burnt, and So You Wanna Talk About How I'm the Dead Girl in the Painting first appeared in *Querencia Press's Anthology*

Bird Shit at Dusk first appeared in *Noctua Review*

And Anyways / And Nevermind first appeared in *Blood Moon POETRY*

Ode to Lost Things first appeared in Crab Creek Review

Woman is the ___th Confirmed Case of a Blood Clot Related to the Vaccine, The First Thirty Days, Ode to My Legs, and Everywhere I look things keep dying first appeared in *Wishbone Words*

Notes

Allison Titus, *sum of every lost ship* (CSU Poetry, Copyright © 2009)

Emily Kendal Frey, *Sorrow Arrow* (Octopus Books, Copyright © 2014)

Natalie Diaz, *Postcolonial Love Poem* (Graywolf Press, Copyright © 2020)

Emily Skaja, *Brute* (Graywolf Press, Copyright © 2019)

Tommy Pico, *FEED* (Tin House Books, Copyright © 2019)

Richard Siken, *War of the Foxes* (Copper Canyon Press, Copyright © 2015)

Olivia Gatwood, *Life of the Party* (Penguin Books, Copyright © 2019)

Billy-Ray Belcourt, *A History of My Brief Body* (Two Dollar Radio, Copyright © 2020)

This collection also references:

Jane the Virgin (2014-2019)

Practical Magic (1998)

Moxie (2021)

Modern Family (2009-2020)

Fleetwood Mac, "Sisters of the Moon" (© 1979)

Thanks

My endless gratitude to Emily Perkovich for taking a chance on another one of my baby books. Thanks to my parents, my siblings, my partner, my dogs (one whom is now looking out for me from some unknown plain), and all my extended family–friends included–who have supported my dreams, bought my books, come to readings, and given me all the love, support, laughter, and commiseration needed to bolster a person living in the hellscape that is late-stage capitalism, a pandemic, massive global extinction, and a burning world. A big giant thanks to Catherine Broadwall for supporting my poetry dreams when I haven't believed in them myself, reading every poem fresh out of the factory of my body and showing them love, and writing a beautiful blurb for this book child. Equally, thanks to Kelly Gray, poet and nature enthusiast, whose work continues to inspire me and who also wrote a stunning blurb for this book. The support of badass women continues to raise me up and I am nowhere, am nothing, without their bodily and writerly uplifting. May our tidal waves of ferocity rise above the land and drown those who would hold us down.

www.ingramcontent.com/pod-product-compliance
Lightning Source LLC
Chambersburg PA
CBHW031246120626
46545CB00007B/2667